The Longest Pleasure

poems by

Vinita Agrawal

Finishing Line Press
Georgetown, Kentucky

The Longest Pleasure

Copyright © 2016 by Vinita Agrawal
ISBN 978-1-944251-20-8 First Edition
All rights reserved under International and Pan-American Copyright Conventions.
No part of this book may be reproduced in any manner whatsoever without written permission from the publisher, except in the case of brief quotations embodied in critical articles and reviews.

ACKNOWLEDGMENTS

Breaking, Looking for Love, Something Somewhere were published in *Raedleaf Poetry India* in August 2013. http://rlpoetry.org/carnival/4-poems-vinita-agrawal/"
November and Home were also published by *Raedleaf Poetry India* in January 2014, http://rlpoetry.org/wp-content/uploads/2014/01/The-Brown-Boat.pdf www.rlp.org
Conversation Inmates was published in *www.sparkthemagazine.com*, July 2014
More Useful was solicited by *FoxChase Review* and published in their Fall Issue, 2015
Sea of Time was published in *www.openroadreview.com* in the November Issue, 2013, http://www.openroadreview.in/sea-of-time-by-vinita-agrawal-india/
Summer We Called Home published in the 2015 Fall Issue of *Pea River Journal*

Editor: Christen Kincaid

Cover Art: Ryan Baumstark

Author Photo: Apurv Agrawal

Cover Design: Elizabeth Maines

Printed in the USA on acid-free paper.
Order online: www.finishinglinepress.com
           also available on amazon.com

Author inquiries and mail orders:
Finishing Line Press
P. O. Box 1626
Georgetown, Kentucky 40324
U. S. A.

Table of Contents

The Windstorm Came in March 1
Pedder Road Flyover 2
Wrought By the Storm 4
Some Things I Knew the Day I Was Born 6
Hide and Seek 7
Jovan Musk and Tiananmen Square 9
Always You 11
Robert and Amaryllis 13
Azadirachta Indica 14
Missing Person 15
Something Somewhere 17
Breaking 18
Looking For Love 19
The Way a Photo Speaks 20
Conversation Inmates 21
November 23
More Useful 24
Sea of Time 25
Home 26
Broken 27
Eye Am 28
Insurgents 29
Time Lag 30
Summer We Called Home 31

*"Now hatred is by far the longest pleasure;
men love in haste but they detest at leisure"*
Lord Byron *(English Romantic poet and satirist, 1788-1824)*

The Windstorm Came In March

and uprooted the rosewood in the forest.
No Morse codes for help were scratched in the mud
no lovers chased the winged seeds erupting from bean pods
You and I were left staring at the blazing red blossoms of the Indian
      coral
that clawed at the skies like a fusillade of bloody tridents.
We were left listening to the silence that followed the storm
ricocheting off boles, rippling off wood chips scattered in the soil,
left dwarfed by huge rain-dimpled trees that had weathered a tempest
I tried to listen to the sap running through their barks
to keep myself from listening to your breathing,
the briskly transported chlorophyll or sucrose
oblivious to threats posed by an axe
hatchet, chain-saw, colored flare or a windstorm...
When I whispered
'how can all this disappear'
you shrugged mildly
and picked up a jagged bit of wind-thrown wood
examined it for losses,
watched it darken in your hand
like a fragment of time.
And I wondered,
how could I possibly not mourn
the severed Sal, Teak, Rosewood, Laburnum,
whenever I mourned the loss of love
after we had parted.

Pedder Road Flyover

It was here
underneath the posh flyover
with its underbelly bursting open like a crammed carton of sins
that I learnt about life.
I saw existence morph from penthouses and slick condos
to the wall-less homes of ragpickers
like a Salvador Dali painting, except for the curation of colors.
Grey was the color here—it was in children's hair,
in men's intentions, inside women's wombs,
between the fault lines of being born poor
and in the meager light of a dawn
that somehow always escaped with the sun.
Women sat in blouses and petticoats
on saris spread out like carpets
combed hair, picked lice, smoked bidis, chewed Areca nuts
reveled in the mild kick of carcinogen numbing their mouths.
They cooked once a day over wood-fired clay stoves
in aluminum pots—rice, added alarming amounts of water when it
      was done.
In the short run, water made the stomach heavy.
Here there were no long runs...
The naked, insect bitten infants looked crimped.
Always begged for the breast, their faces wan with hunger
that they shouldn't have ever known. Ideally.
Here they lived—under the canopy of opulence
on a road named after Mr. W.G. Pedder,
a British Municipal Commissioner of 1879 Bombay.
Politicians changed the name to Dr. G. Deshmukh Marg after a social
      reformer.
But somehow the families here still picked garbage,
waded around in stench, did death's work,

stayed alive only because cholera was dead.
If you ventured out at the devil's hour,
you'd have heard them groan into the darkness
as at last, traffic dimmed around three in the morning.
A few hours of oblivion must have felt good
with loyal street dogs curled up warmly by their sides.

Wrought By the Storm

We sat by the window
shuddering like panes at the howling winds
Peering at the clouds tossed about helplessly
like bed rolls at the mercy of a squall.
Boughs whinnied like wild mares forcibly reined.
The furious magma of the storm flooded our ears.

The storm struck our prayer bell
Shook the Gods at the altar
Caused the fan to whir anti-clockwise
Jerked wildly in our pulse beats
Skewed our outer expressions of calm
Flickered like fear in our eyes

'I miss your pigtails', father quirked,
Your bloodcurdling screams in weather like this.
'Your calligraphy of Chinese alphabets
on damp windows to ward off the storm dragons.'

'Only Laughing Buddhas don't grow up!'
I reparteed.

After our smiles had faded
left our eyes,
we acknowledged in silence
how we missed mother's presence.
She would have outwitted the fierce conditions by now
would have stuffed one of her old muslin saris
in the crevices of French windows
and muffled the screeching breeze.
Checked every glass pane for loose rubber gaskets.
Outsmarted the wailing outside
with a smartly whistling kettle of hot tea.
But she wasn't here.

She was immune from geography now,
beyond the nautical
cocooned in some natural state
that no air could stir.

I got up with intent
went about doing
what mother would have done.
Carried a tray of tea back to Father
as we mended the cracks
wrought by the storm
in gentle silence.

Some Things I Knew the Day I Was Born

I'd craft phrases
To please your delicate ego

Never tell you what I really thought or how I felt
only what you wished to hear

I'd disappear inside my home
nor you or the children would care to look for me

I'd nurture modest dreams, mildly defining who I was
but not in a way that might threaten your kingdom

I'd dress demurely, cover my legs and shoulders
curb the desires marbling somewhere around my navel

I'd choke on my own wild silence
on some dark nights of stark solitude

Being born female is a crime
I'd be so soundless that I might not be at all

Worst of all, duplicity would be my greatest talent
hypocrisy and fakery my biggest virtues

So it would go on, without respite
everyday—a blank page

Some things I knew the day I was born

Hide and Seek

He was a paw.
A city-bred shark.
Eyes beady like black stamens of scarlet poppies.
Skin greasy with diabolical adulthood.
When little girls in the neighborhood vanished,
Mother forbade us from wearing hair bands, bobby clips
and accepting candies from strangers.
We saw peccant phantoms on staircases, terror teeth in parks
felt angina like fear in our chests on deserted roads
Lust was a saliva glinting bubble
Lust was the nigella blackness of fingernails

Mother said he was single dimensional
Tricky as the weather
Cheap as plastic
With a wind chime voice.
Dogs hated him—
raised hackles when he passed by.
Tuberculate shoe buckles
became the focus of our eyes.
We daren't look up at all—
doves were extinct. Vultures ruled.
Lust was a rough shoulder blade
a razor, a miter, a chicken wing, a priest
our pinafores, a game of hide and seek… it was anything.

Despite all, he cornered us once;
in our checked school uniforms.
Said he was a game developer.
Despite all, we blushed and giggled.
Not quite sure of...what?
Tamarind and raw mangoes churned in our stomachs.
We stared as his arms morphed,
squid-like, into eight tentacles.
We screamed. We ran. That afternoon we ran.
Ran till we met the skies
Lust was a rainbow slashing the heavens.
Lust was the first weak breath returning to our lungs.

Jovan Musk and Tiananmen Square

It's strange how I remember nothing of the Tiananmen Square
    incident
I was twenty four when it occurred and a student of political science
So ideally, I ought to have been a part of it
Through articles, pamphlets, through sheer outrage, if nothing else
Yet I remember nothing of it

I remember instead
Thinking deeply about the way my fiancé's lashes curled
And how soft and respectful his voice was
Those blue inland letters he wrote in a neat, straight hand
I remembered his crisp white shirts on square shoulders
Liberally sprayed with Jovan Musk

He wasn't the kind who'd stop using Musk perfumes
Simply because Musk Deer were going extinct
Being brutally hunted in the Himalayas for their scented pods
And I wasn't the kind (then) to mind it either
So, with such a mind, I remembered nothing of Tiananmen Square

Twenty five years later my marriage and the massacre of Tiananmen
Are both celebrating their silver jubilees;
The cruel suppression of protests of unarmed individuals
Stifling free expression and the courage of speech
The right to association and assembly…dissent against trials and
    censorship

Today, with the rains beating like drums against my windows,
I pull out an old trunk from college days
Dig out scores of folders, files, loose sheets of paper full of words
There they are! In a folder marked June 1989
My passionate objections to the Chinese atrocities at the City square

Published in newspapers and periodicals,
Proving that I hadn't been indifferent after all
Just that I had forgotten amidst Jovan Musks and Baby Smells
The screams of raw blood flooding a public street
Unaware, that on its silver jubilee, I'd be reminded with deadly hurt
Of what it was like to live in oppression's long shadow

Always You

It was you all the way, my love,
right from the days we dangled
on adventitious air roots of the banyan tree
till all things herbaceous died down to the ground
in the last autumn of life, it was you. Only you.

You taught me the subtleties of life
through Ferns, Succulents, Woody Evergreens, Annuals...
Some living on...leafless forever,
some dying back until a new season arrived. Each one true to its
       Genus.

You taught me how to inhale the scent of peonies from a photograph
by whipping up images of mulch, roots, sunlight and breeze
taught me the humility of wrangled branches
that hosted glossy hairless leaves.

Songs of abandonment I heard in apple blossoms,
the silent melody of earth through soil up to its neck in flowers,
complete stillness through gales surrendering to valleys
to then disappear forever.

Love was as simple as a rustic four-petal rose growing wild.
It smelled like mountain mist lobbed in pine cone tassels.
As warm as native violets and golden poppies,
sitting in a vase on a table for two.

Your eyes were a cinnamon ocean—fragrant like hearth
where all my rivers met, where I merged at dusk
to lay calm at night. The same night
that made wet rot out of people, turned them to fuzzy spores.

Sometimes when cold and chill claimed my heart
and the world became leathery and elliptical,
you held my hand, showed me nymphs hiding inside daffodils
so that I laughed...and then you laughed with me.

Robert and Amaryllis

We were both nine then when old uncle Ash gifted me
an Indoor Grow Kit of Amaryllis. I ran over to your house
and we got excited about having something to plant and watch over.

We placed the box of sandy loam
in partial shade by the dining room window.
You came by every evening after school to watch life burgeoning
      from a kit.

Then one day in early spring, a cluster of buds emerged at the helm
of the light green stem.
Although right then they only looked like potato "eyes",
they squeezed our hearts with joy.

A month later the deep red, funnel shaped blooms trumpeted out.
Shining in our eyes, blushing at our delighted whoops!
That day we held hands. Mother baked us a cake.

Your father got posted to the Embassy of Bhutan.
You left in a week's time. We cried. You told me how much you hated
leaving the beautiful Amaryllis that we'd grown together.

I wiped your tears with my fingers, tasted them surreptitiously.
Later, you sent me a leaflet on how to preserve seeds by sewing them
and how to dry out bulbs for a new season.

We never met again but I have to say that every time I cried,
you came back to me—tasting of air in a mountain kingdom
stirring in the heart of a blood red Amaryllis.

Azadirachta Indica

Have you ever sat under the shade of Margosa?
Was it after you learned that it was a killer?
Anti everything that didn't deserve to live—
bacteria, virus, fungus, pests, mites, ticks
septic, acne, anxiety, insomnia...even sperms.
Medicinal king. Every Indian courtyard has one.

Have you chewed one in the morning?
Toothbrush sticks that village folk use.
Scrubby. Dark brown. Unsweetened.
A relentless guardian until the next light of dawn.

Dr. Shastri took me for a walk the other day
on a nameless road with overwhelming neem scents
released from serrated magic leaves
purifying the afternoon like good intentions.

Watch, he said, and picked up a golden yellow seed
popped it between his thumb and forefinger until oil oozed out.
He poured it on a worm down below, stunning it.
It retreated hastily. Didn't stand a chance.

Later, I dipped my sins in it,
hoping it would cauterize tissues of guilt
sterilize thorny voices in my head
that accused me of being unclean.

Missing Person

I don't remember anything about the day we emptied mother's ashes
    in the river.
Just the overcast grey sky, dowelled like a Serengeti of gloom
    somewhere up above.

The hospital had trussed her hermetically to prevent chemical
    bloating,
scaffolded her abdomen in particular...too much tumor there, they'd
    said blandly.
So, in the end, that's how she had lain on the pyre
and breathed in our hearts.

Her cork-soled slippers had waited patiently in the corner of her
    room
the way an old woman awaits the return of her son gone to war.
I'd hoarded in my cupboard her lemon sari—the one that she'd worn
    for the last time,
like a chipmunk stashing acorns for a bleak winter.

Even now it's easy to see her—
the tiny scar on her brow, her satin eyes
one front harp-shaped tooth in a row of perfect others
her chiffon cheeks, those smiling lips,
the chemo ravaged hair and cuticles...

We'd lied to her everyday;
assured her that she'd recover.
What did she tell herself, I wonder.
When the stone cold moon paused at her window by night
and stars glimmered transparently over the darkness like sweat, what
    demons did she confront?
Did she remember to pledge herself to us again for the next life?

On the third day, we emptied her ashes into the thick belly of a
　　　swiftly flowing river.
Lacing cold, turbulent foam with warm eternal peace...
our cheeks as pale as skeletons,
our grief as dark as the mountains in the far horizons
sprayed against grey skies, brutally pegging a day to the calendar.
A day that had a date, a month, a year and one missing person.

Something Somewhere

Something, something must be left behind
We must have left a trace at least
of our bond

warm it was
like the skin between entwined fingers
like the sun shining out of eyes

We'd spun endless strings
to keep us entwined forever
If only we hadn't let go of the beginning

If not the skeins, the knots must be somewhere
Lying hidden on the jungles of floors, like traps
to trip new lovers.

I remember your every breath
lining the quad of my world,
Now those breaths are leasing life to a daisy, magnolia or lily, I'm sure

How can meanings disappear
from destiny's designs
even if we foolishly flout every sign

What once was, can never be again.
But nothingness throbs with a life of its own
It sculpts a new you.

When all is gone, nothingness must remain
If only to prove that what was real once
is debris and rubble now.

Breaking

My future lovers mean nothing to me
This anguish has wiped me out
Scattered me into the invisible winds
I am not food for even the birds
My scars run deep between faith and God
Right now, I don't even know how to love myself
I opiate between me and my distances
If you can, do only this for me;
Absolve me of being born a woman
Else leave me alone on some untrodden path
With my missing heartbeats.

Looking for Love

My hunger for love
has started to fill the air
I can now hold sunlight with my teeth
and bytes and gigabytes with my arms
It makes no difference that the tubes of New York
are clogged with water or that Mumbai is
drowning in the rains
so long as the surfing freeways are clear.
My brain will take anything you give me
anything to take the place of love
Even cyber skin.

The Way a Photo Speaks

I have a picture on my wall of a Pa-O woman
selling vegetables in the by lanes of Yangon, Burma.
Greens and tubers meticulously arranged on a jute sack-cloth
butter beans, asparagus, bamboo shoots, Asiatic penny wort,
She squats in the mud, head covered with a red checked scarf
her eyes squinting mildly at the sky as she lives her culture
through kafir lime, lemon grass, mustard greens and okra.

The shot sags a bit in that nebulous space between sky and earth
where satellite cables criss-cross the air
like snake markings on the skin of the atmosphere.
Even through that mess, I can see a tureen of raffish clouds,
their bellies heavy with the moisture of the Irrawaddy river ready to
 serve rain.
The streets of Burma are seldom dry. Water and blood are shed
 equally.

Above the market square hangs a notice board
written in a Brahmi like script, nailed to a wooden scaffold
holding up a crumbling colonial structure.
I used to think nothing of it until a Burmese friend walked in
one day and read it for me
Said, it's a notice of the Communist Party of Burma—CPB
saying "Hard to join, Easy to Quit".

I don't know why I have the picture on my wall
Don't know the woman's name
But I know she has sons out there
in the military junta
Every night she lights butter lamps for their return
begs the earth to yield not beans and asparagus
but peace, peace, peace.

Conversation Inmates

Conversation is origami
a clever two sided sheet
crafting swans, mansions, vultures
out of nothing
in a train or plane
when your head is jumble of hellos and goodbyes

Conversation is a vestment
a metal habit reserved by fathers
for sons caught sleeping late
daughters caught partying late
mothers are bridges between words and silence
a subway to the relief of a room

Conversation is water
gurgling like hungry stomachs between friends
tumbling awkwardly like a new-born calf between
relatives
flowing silently between you and your dog
stagnating between a couple growing apart
sparkling like champagne for a beau

Conversation is a walk in the woods
contemplating your worn boots
feeling the mist, soaking the rain
missing a warm hand
doodling in the mud with a stick
a nervous twitch of silence

Conversation is a stutter
swallowing hurt, hurting with swallowing
a faltering smile, an apology
a mile etched out on a six foot bed
a lizard sulking on the wall, eyeing all
a morning that's as plastic as the night

Conversation is buckwheat
starching interviews, nourishing bosses;
dusting glass ceilings, flavorless as a drone
energizing as a game of Chinese checkers
worse still, chess,
a cover crop designed to checkmate.

November

November is in my lap like an old shoe
Nowhere to walk, nowhere to go
Tattered, torn, worn, abandoned
Lonely like a forgotten imprint sinking in the sands of time

November is in my lap like a scraggly wet bird
Shivering, burrowing in my thighs for warmth
When the sun comes out, I will teach it to fly
Until then it gazes me with terrified eyes, makes me cry

November is a milestone
Gathering my surrender in lonely miles
Making an autumn heap of promises, a bonfire of hopes
Its face is creased and wrinkled, its face is blue

More Useful

Why can't I be chopped like a tree
Torso falling to the ground in obeisance
For the nurture

Dying and drying in the sun
Limbs like branches
Torn by passersby for firewood
Eyes like leaves
Settling into the top layer of soil
Humus and moisture
Food for worms and insects

Such a death would be more useful
Than this imitation life

Sea of Time

In the mornings
I am nameless, faceless

a patchwork of bits of yesterday
appliquéd to a floating tomorrow

Hopes make a soft fistula between the
fingers I keep crossed for today

Sunlight arrives like therapy
Yet, darkness lingers in the iris, in the spine

Moments are dust
to be shaken off and floated

with riverine intentions
into the sea of time

Home

Homes have no walls
no rooms, no furniture, no thresholds
Nothing through which you might enter
and nothing from which you might want to exit
Because homes are not houses

Homes are built in the eyes
Erected by naked, hungry hearts
In skies, in dew drops, lichen, mosses,
Sometimes on parched, parted lips
Sometimes inside the darkening irises of your eyes

Homes are tender assembles of empty air
Sorted by the linear breaths you lend to me;
Built for unborn little feet to run
And for smiles to sun themselves on broad porticos

My home is in the centre of your palms
Sunk in the wells of your destiny
That you carry like a liquid in your eyes
Or like an abode in your hand, my very own delta
Between the nine mounds of the universe

Broken

This broken home is like a chopped tree trunk
Showing rings of life ruthlessly axed

Leaving behind an upturned patellar face of pain
Breath broken in a cinch

Its lode of warmth is plundered
Rime's leftovers straggle the trashcan like cold meat

I sense the condors circling above, in my bones
As they scavenge for the rich, juicy morsels of a home, now dead

The aged wind is weary of reviving fires so often doused
It's shoulders too weak to carry ashes heavy with severing

So this is how things break in this world
This is how hope loses altitude

There must be someone to blame
There must also be someone who will lead me back to myself

Eye Am

Come nearer
Let me show you the age around my eyes
and the very little time they have left, to hold their shape.

The decrepit warehouse of the retina
Where happiness has been long out of stock.
The smooth, white sclera, hopelessly dinted from within by brown
    singing mountains.

The bleak, slow compass of the sun at its corners
making thin furrows from earth's gloss
to plant seeds squinting with pain, amidst constant rain.

Every lash swording salt crystals,
conserving moisture, sheathing the aqueous
from rubble images that brought existence to the level of the feet.

The deep-diving corneas that scavenged your lips for promises
where there were none, for words where there were none.
Pincering membranes of silence, listening to nothing.

If I could, I'd show you the squiggly floaters,
the sloughed off debris swimming in the vitreous humor,
giving shapes to days first thing in the morning, like symbolic zodiac
    charts.

Come nearer, so you don't miss the scheme of translucence and
    opacity.
The flecks of sherry brown in a pool of liquid coal
like tiny amber ribbons tied to life whenever someone cared to say
    my name.

Insurgents

You're not here, can't ask you about the look on your face
as you escaped that Bilboes summer of 1965,
your mottled irises, your sweaty upper lips,
the skitter of skeletons I hear in your ear even if it's just a painting.

Gun powder raids the air, I can tell
by his hand gripping yours,
your bodies quailing against the felt tipped Escambray mountains.
The Pico San Juan gleaming silver this moonlight, guarding the valley
    of sugar mills.

Regimes chase out even air; your low patio walls would never have
    kept it out.
God knows which village you made it to, which peasant gave you
    bread.
God knows by which river you caught your breath,
smiled at each other through burning charcoal eyes.

Your footsteps, soft as a calf's underbelly,
stumbling over tree stumps, boulders, spittle and grass,
sprawling, racing towards an awning of freedom—
lie concealed in the mystery of the artwork.

You did it for your land...your paradise,
for the courage of your convictions
and in some corner of my heart, I believe,
also, for love.

Time Lag

Despite loess caressing the roots
and the damp, earthy aroma of trees,
a brokenness clings to the winds;
fresh as a pistil that has just lost its flower.
Despite the wet tissues made of air and rain,
the tree branches look fractured
their leaves pale like pinched skin.
Despite the ordination of the sun
into the earth's stratosphere,
despite the steady respiration of porous limestones,
a lag claims my chest—
the same lag that tender shoots feel
before they acquire the austere ankles of trees that see them through
    storms.
The same lag that silhouettes endure just before dawn
before daylight makes them real.
The lag that dilated pupils suffer under bright light
see nothing, feel all
as though eyes were contoured to a painful illumination,
blinded...before starting to see again.

Summer We Called Home

Unfulfilled promises jangle like an empty syringe of morphine
Sprinkling the pain of blockages further into the veins

The chapel at the turn of the street is cob-webbed with morbid
    confessions
They tar its facade; reduce it to a box of walls when faith disappears

I cannot pray anymore...I am sunk in the creek, in a jungle of letting-go
When rescued, I'll make triangular boats and float them in your name,
    like water flags

Seasons will come and go and I will continue to sing the songs you
    wrote for me
From between the jowls of my December mufflers...

...Will continue to torch the corners that failed to receive light
In the spell binding, fleeting, summer of our love...a summer we
    called home

Author of *Words Not Spoken*, Vinita is a Mumbai based, award winning poet and writer. Her poems have appeared in *Asiancha, Constellations, The Fox Chase Review, Pea River Journal, Open Road Review, Stockholm Literary Review, Poetry Pacific* and over a 100 other national and international journals. She was nominated for the Best of the Net Awards 2011, awarded first prize in the Wordweavers Contest 2014, commendation prize in the All India Poetry Competition 2014 and won the 2014 Hour of Writes Contest thrice. Her poems have found a place significant national anthologies like *Suvarnarekha* and *Dance with the Peacocks* in several international anthologies compiled in Australia. Recently, she was co judge for the Asian Cha Poetry Contest 2015. She has given readings at two SAARC events in Delhi and Agra. She also read her poetry at Hyderabad at an event organized by the U.S. Consulate to celebrate the Women Poets Of India. She also read for Delhi Poetree where twenty four of her poems were compiled in an anthology titled *WordWine* and at Cappucino Readings, Mumbai an eclectic platform showcasing poets from all over India.

www.ingramcontent.com/pod-product-compliance
Lightning Source LLC
Chambersburg PA
CBHW051705040426
42446CB00009B/1308